# THE PEOPLE WHO DIDN'T SAY GOOD-BYE

✸ ✸ ✸ ✸

# THE PEOPLE WHO DIDN'T SAY GOOD- BYE

## MERRIT MALLOY

A DOLPHIN BOOK

DOUBLEDAY & COMPANY, INC.,
GARDEN CITY, NEW YORK

Library of Congress Cataloging in Publication Data

Malloy, Merrit.
The people who didn't say good-bye.

I. Title.
PS3563.A4318P4   1984      811'.54
ISBN 0-385-18784-X (a Dolphin book : pbk.)

"A Dolphin book."

Designed by Virginia M. Soulé

ISBN # 0-385-18784-X
Library of Congress Catalog Card Number: 82-45932
Copyright © 1985 by Merrit Malloy

For J.M. Barrie and the lost boys

# CONTENTS

# THE PEOPLE WHO DIDN'T SAY GOOD-BYE

◉ ◉ ◉ ◉

# A NOTE FROM THE AUTHOR

This is just a book of words
It is an instrument of crossing
One of the hands is yours

Communication
is a
partnership

Each of you who reads these words
will rewrite
them

Poetry is always
a
collaboration

We can turn walls into windows
And these are just words

# THE PEOPLE WHO
# CANNOT SAY GOOD-BYE

There are people who cannot say good-bye
They are born this way/this is how they die
They are the keepers of promises/what moves them does
   not wear out
Their loyalty will tear apart your clocks

These are the people who can hear the music in songs
They are the Vow carriers
The grandmothers who always leave the porchlight on
No one is lost to the one who sees

These are the women widowed by men they never
   married
These are the girls who wait even when you don't come
These are the mothers of orphans/They can turn a fake
   into an original
They will hear the prayer in your self-contempt

As distance is measured/people do not end
It is one of those stories that cannot be written down
except across a lifetime of open doors
There is a holding on beyond the letting go
There is a reunion in everybody's chest
This is how we come to make a family from strangers
This is how we light candles

There are people who will remember you when you meet
   them
These are the people you can always call at night

They are humans turned angels by your asking
With each separation they go to seed again

These are the men who carried you on their shoulders
This is the one you are lonely for
the one who begins and ends your hunger
This is the man who said 'Always'

There is a moment of returning on the other side of every
    leaving
It is not something I can prove to you in language
This is what we pray about
. . . We can kill what we desire
and it grows back

There is something that does not wear out
It is the third part of any two people who join
It opens and closes

There are people alone who are not apart
This is why we listen to the madman when he speaks
People change but they do not stop
This is how we learn 'Forever'

There are people you can count on/They are the keepers
    of promises
They are candles lit from each other
They can teach us eternity
We can get what we give/This is the instruction
There are people who do not say good-bye
As distance is measured
You are one of them

❋ ❋ ❋ ❋

# THE HOLY PART

Love is not one action
it is the holy part

Love isn't just doing good things
it is the spirit with which we do good things

You draw hearts
but love is a
combination

And my telling you this instead of putting my arms
   around you
is how I can miss the holy point

❀ ❀ ❀ ❀

## BASIC MATH

I'm old-fashioned
I still believe that people
can stay married
for the rest of their lives
as long as they do it
with one person
at a time

# SOMETHING YOU CAN COUNT ON

I want to tell you
in a few words
what I could not tell you
in too many

I want you to know
that it will be hard
to live without you
again

You will always be the one
I'm thinking about
when somebody asks me
who I'm thinking
about

☼ ☼ ☼ ☼

## ONE OF THE FIRST THINGS
## WE HAVE TO LEARN

No matter how long she held on
to those people she lost
No matter how hard she tried
to get them back
Not one of them ever
returned to her

We must be careful
not to relinquish our future
to people who won't
be there

One of the first things
we have to let go of
is *not* being able to
let go of
anybody

## DETERMINATION

Persistence can (sometimes) make things last
But it doesn't always
make things
work

The muscle will harden
wherever you give
it exercise
But

Endurance isn't always
enough . . . Because

Practice can make anything
perfect
. . . Even grief can become
an art

# IMPERFECTIONS

Why is it that you wanted me more on
the night I was leaving
than you ever wanted me
before?

Does pain bring people
closer together than
pleasure?

Are we more afraid of
living together than of
dying alone

Does distance unite people more deeply
than familiarity?

It is as though our hunger
is to be hungry and
our real need is
to be missed

It's no accident that the songs
that sell the most
are sad

## VALENTINE'S DAY

It was Valentine's Day
Another Christmas for lovers
He thought surely he would hear from her tonight
(she loved him so when they played that song)
So he built himself a winter fire
and waited by the phone

It was Valentine's Day
So she bought fresh flowers at the market
and she poured jasmine in her bath this afternoon
She thought surely he would find her on a night like this
"I'll always love you in February,"
he used to say

They both stayed home
on the fourteenth of February this year
Each was hoping the other would call by now
But the familiar theme from *The Tonight Show*
reminded them that the night
was closing

He was certain she was with somebody else
Her Irish hair in somebody else's hands
He felt so old that he wore socks
to bed

And she felt so cold that she turned the
electric blanket up to nine and
let the dog sleep
on the bed

They both took a sleeping pill
and were asleep before Johnny brought out
his first guest

# THE DAY HE TOOK THIS PICTURE

The day he took this picture
he loved me

And I don't know how to show you
what I mean . . . Except to say
that I don't look like this
anymore

This is how I used to look
when he loved
me

# JUNGLE MOVES

Your leaving
is not so perfect
that it makes me a stranger
again

When you see me with other men
You will always pull back
like the boy gripping his sandpail
yelling "Mine!" "Mine!"
"Mine!"

No man ever grows so old
that he can bear with comfort
the sight of another mouth
at his
nipple

❀ ❀ ❀ ❀

# THE LONG WAY HOME

Why is it when
people feel they are losing
each other they always leave
each other?

Why do people
walk away from their houses
when all they ever have
to do to get home
is turn
around?

✿ ✿ ✿ ✿

## SOMETHING TO THINK ABOUT

There was a time when I didn't know you . . . And
I didn't miss you then
at all

## OLD BEN

"Even though he's been gone a dozen winters
I still worry about
him when the roads
are bad"

She leaned back in the chair
and took me back through the quarter century
they spent trying to say good-bye to each other
"Mary, I wish I could tell you
that it doesn't hurt anymore"
Huge human tears fell down across
her smile
She closed her eyes and
I could almost see him come up out of her memory
"He used to kiss me right here on the back
of the neck" . . . Her fingers were on that spot
where his mouth used to be

I felt my heart break exactly
where hers was
broken

"Ben . . . good old Ben
he's one of those men that you can't lose
he grows back," she said
as only she could say it
"He's gone away so many times before
but he always shows up somewhere"

"You can't lose men like Ben enough"
and she took my hand like you used to do

Surely he was here with her tonight
I saw her as only Ben could have seen her . . .
It was one of those songs that nobody sings
and the words still make you cry

❀ ❀ ❀ ❀

## WHAT NOBODY EVER DID

Everybody who ever said
"Nobody will ever love you
like I do"
was right
. . . Nobody ever did

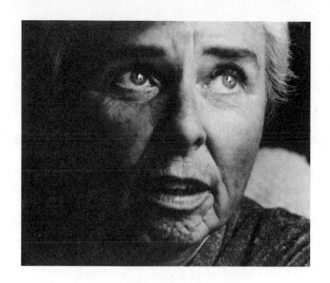

## CONSIDERATIONS

How thoughtful of you not to come over
and point out my loneliness
with an invitation
to dinner

You have distinguished me
with your affectionate
silence
. . . Your voice became more remarkable
the more you chose not
to speak

You did not come to me (as others have)
with theatrical kindness
. . . You did not use my grief

as an opportunity
to compare your own
sorrow . . . No

You stayed your friendly distance
assuming my pain did not need
a guardian . . . and you were closer to me
than any who came with open arms
forcing me to review my life
and detail its
tragedy

My dear friend
How thoughtful of you to give me support
and not help
And how wise you are
to know the
difference

# CHOICES

All you have to do
to change your life
is to change your mind
. . . It really is that simple
But it isn't always
easy

All you have to do to
stop feeling bad
is to start feeling
good . . . but

'Feeling good' is not a
onetime event
It is a decision we make
minute by minute
day by day
. . . It is a creation

The way to change the world
is to change your attitude
towards it
. . . not just once
but all the
time

# DELIVERANCE

If a man moves you to feel
like a woman
. . . the least you can do is
let him

You must never let your fear of God
keep you out of
Heaven

## FIRE AGAINST FIRE

My body is asking me
to take a chance
on someone

I move impatiently
towards a lover
I haven't met

He will enter my mouth
and shove you back into
my memory

Only a man
can cure a woman
of a man

✱ ✱ ✱ ✱

## HEAT

I'm afraid of what
you'll do to me . . . But
I'm more afraid
that you might not
do it

## INGREDIENTS

So confused by the original
they only sang
on Sunday

The mystery is that there is
no mystery

Things mean what you want them
to mean

You can get what you give
this is the instruction
the trick is not to tell the story
like it wasn't about you

The secret is there is
no secret

I can only tell you what I see
not what was seen—
the eyes are original work

## MIGRATIONS

There is no photograph of that November that includes
the two of us and
I won't tempt language to tell you
any more than this

We used each other up
in three and a half weeks
it was a romantic crisis
one long accident of desire
it was (probably) a
miracle . . . But

Passion isn't love
and
Fire isn't the source of
light

As any magician can prove
Romance is a
trick . . . So

I've come to remember him in a scotch plaid muffler
(I don't know if he's ever had one)
I can still see him walking down Sixth Avenue
the muffler waving out like a long arm
there is a moment (even now) when I don't know
if he was walking towards me
or away

## PREYING

Everybody thinks
they're the only one . . . And Everybody
is right
and
wrong

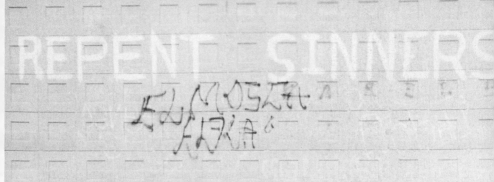

## INVITATIONS

He's afraid of her
She's a victim
. . . She is inviting him
to be a criminal

It is part of the
plan . . . She wants to
ruin him in *self-defense*

She's a victim
and
Killers are afraid of her
Because

She *lets* them
kill

✻ ✻ ✻ ✻

## TWICE A BEGGAR

It's something we all
wish for and
something we're all
afraid of

. . . To feel nothing when
it hurts and
To feel everything
when it
doesn't

## THE WAY MY FATHER
## LOOKED AT MY MOTHER

There was a way my Father looked at my Mother
. . . It is the way that men look at women
I didn't want to . . . But
I saw it

There was an intimacy that
orphaned me . . . It was brief and
dangerous and so beautiful that even
children cannot talk about it

There was a way they held on to each other
that left no room in their arms for me
. . . It is that erotic sacrament that turns children
into strangers

They would lock the bedroom door
leaving me with my brothers
in that particular exile we shared
at the bottom of
the stairs

There was a 'way' my Mother was with my Father
It is the way that women are with men
There was a place of loyalty where
she always knew him
first

There was a separate place where they were together
a holy region where they were not at all
mine

There was a way my Father looked at my Mother
It is the way that you look at me
It is brief and dangerous and so beautiful
that I have not ever dared to write
it down

## PROPINQUITY

There's a reason
why I can't resist a man
who really loves
children

. . . It's because he has
already loved me once
before

✹ ✹ ✹ ✹

## EARNINGS

There were lots of times
when they didn't think
they'd make it

Nights when they
would lie awake
just holding
on

And often
when the babies were little
they thought about
leaving each other
But . . . they
wouldn't

Later
When they could have
they didn't
So

'In for a penny, in for a pound,'
my Nana used to say
. . . *The secret to staying together*
*is to stay*
*together*

# THE LAST OF
# THE GREAT ROMANTICS

It was always him
even before his name was in my mouth
I could feel his coat hung
over mine

He isn't Irish and
He doesn't have a limp
It is something I gave him
in the story

He is that lost thing
that I cannot
find

We are the two that Sondheim writes about
He is the patriot
I am the girl who
waves

It was always him
even when it could have been
anybody

I will be with him
the last time he looks
at the
sky

I am that lost thing
that he cannot
find

The last thing about me
is the first thing he saw
. . . No one part of me
is missing

# SOCIAL SECURITIES

It's easy to grow old
All you have to do is
go on living . . . But

If you want to grow old together
You have to do it *with*
somebody

## NOTES ON A 'LEG & ASS' MAN

By instinct
you do not trust
. . . You came out of New York with both
fists up
prepared for people to
disappoint you and they
didn't let you
down

You wanted success most of all
because money was the god of your Father
. . . You wanted to place your salvation
in the opinion of
strangers

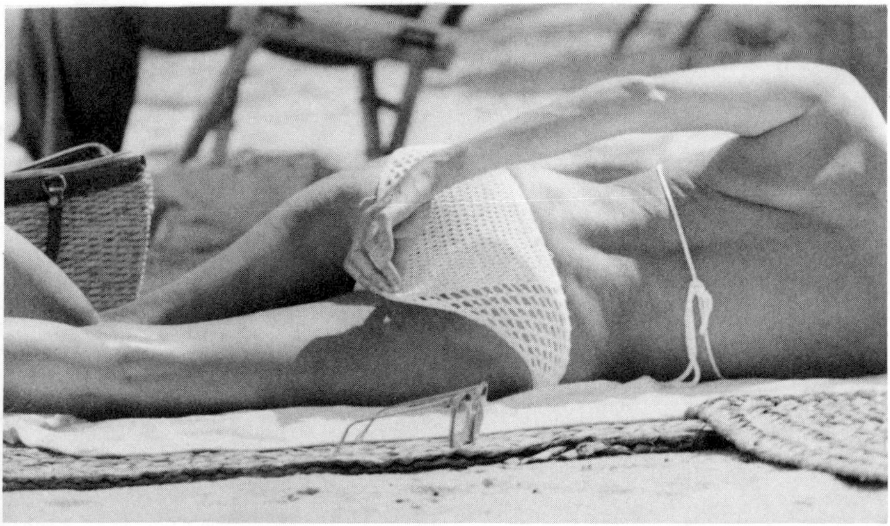

You chose fame
Something that can be given and taken
rather than honor
which can be neither

You chose the safety of cash
(something you can touch) over
the comfort of integrity
(something you can feel)

. . . Is it any mystery that at fifty-seven
you're still afraid of dying poor?

You want God to be there now,
Don't you?

◎ ◎ ◎ ◎

# THE WORKING MAN

He worries a lot about income
as though money had anything to do with poverty
as though dollars could heal him
where he was poor

He says he's working for his children
but his work prevents him from being with them
and he can't figure out why
they're not grateful

He used to talk about it
when he could still feel
back before selfishness made thieves
of everyone . . . And now

He's afraid that he might die
so he's killing himself with work
and just to be safe (in case he doesn't)
He keeps a woman on the side . . . So
He's halfway here and halfway there and
always halfway
home . . . So

He worries a lot about money
as though cash had anything to do with income
He leaves his family to surrogate arms and
fast food

He's proud that he never cheats in business
and God knows he's loyal
The question is to whom?

It's a real talent to succeed
without getting
ahead

## THE MAINTENANCE MAN

There was once a man
who left the girl he married to be with
'the girl he loved'

In return for 'growing old'
with his wife . . . He gave her
money and promises of
maintenance

His guilt made a beggar out of him
(a generous one) . . . So he worked
so hard that he grew old
*for* her instead of
*with* her . . . You see

The man left his wife
because he could not bear
the 'guilt' of 'wanting the
girl he loved' . . .
And now he's leaving 'the girl
he loves' because he cannot bear
the guilt of leaving the
'girl he married'

And so . . . two women are left
without the same man
the maintenance
man

## LIFE GUARDS

Why can't you love someone
who won't love you
first?

Is your heart left
in Brooklyn in some
old competition?

Do your fists rise up
at *me* now for the anger
you felt for *her*
then?

Is it only boys
who were beaten
who grow to men
without
mercy?

How much kindness
will it take to heal
your childhood?

How many times will you
have to hurt *me* before
she stops hurting
*you?*

## THE PETER PRINCIPLE REVISITED

I did not come to you to be
'your wife' but to
'be myself'

I never asked you for your name
. . . I have my own
I could no more change it
to your name than
you could change your name
to mine . . . So

Let me be your love
. . . It is quite enough for me
to 'be myself' with you
than to be 'your wife'
with them

※ ※ ※ ※

## WHAT HE HASN'T LEARNED
## FROM EXPERIENCE

He's not going to say good-bye
It's inconvenient as hell
. . . It is also going to break
every single heart he's ever had
even the last one (the one he was
going to give her if she died
before him) . . . So

No
He's not going to let her go
He's not going to let her
do to him
what he's already done
to her

## THE WAR FOR PEACE

He'll tell you
that we loved each other deeply
but that I fought
too much . . . And
that's true . . . I
did

I didn't make it easy
I wouldn't let him change
that part of me that he loved
and feared and
I wouldn't let him deny
that part of him that
I saw and
wanted

I did fight, that's true
but I didn't fight *with* him
. . . I fought *for* him
and maybe I fought so hard and so much
that it changed his feelings
about me . . . but better that
than it change my feelings
about
myself

❀ ❀ ❀ ❀

# FAILING UPWARDS

I never needed your money
that was a mistake
Poverty would have endeared me to you
dependent as I might
be . . . and

Making my own living was an error, too
"That was *your* job," you said . . .
In taking care of myself I had
robbed you of that pleasure . . . or more clearly
that control (there are other reasons
why women wait at home for men)

I did not ask that you
take care *of* me But
only that you care *for* me
. . . there is quite a difference
in the two

And I never needed your success or fame
the little I had I earned myself
and it displeased you that
I did not need more . . . it confused you
that I did not need yours . . . But, don't you see

I never looked to you as a savior
You were quite enough
as a man

I didn't ask that you
take care *of* me But
only that you care *for* me
. . . there is quite a difference
in the two

The first assumes that I need *help*
and the second only
*love*

# THE IMPORTANCE OF WINGS

He thinks marriage will make our love more real
when marriage will only make our love
more necessary

Staying together is not a sport
It is not some time challenge that marriage
will discipline

Marriage (often)
is just a publicity stunt
a social security
The greatest loves (by no accident)
avoid it . . . So

Yes, I will stay with you
But you don't 'have to' marry me
Marriage is not a payment or something
you can 'give' me
It is not something that you can do 'for' me
only 'with' me

Marriage (I think)
is that odd sacrament that happens privately
when two people arrive at that place
where they already
are

It is not so much a union
as a 'reunion'

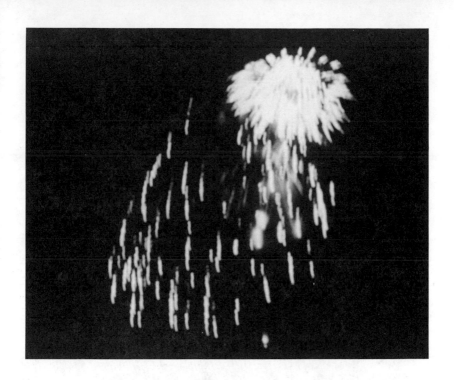

## REVELATIONS

There's a funny thing about
clarity
. . . It can only happen to you
after you've been
confused

In order to be captured
we must first be
free

## NATIVE DANCERS

You know you'll be back . . . So
where are you
going?

Is leaving me
the only way you have of finding out
how much I want you
to stay?

# DOUBLE IMITATION

Leave me in the morning
. . . You left me enough
tonight

You'll be with me
anyway
So why not
stay

I'll close the light
and pretend you're one of the men
I'm going to meet
someday . . . One of those men
I won't be able to
care about

I will imagine you
as one of the men who
I will some night imagine
is you

It will be a double imitation
a three-part harmony
An original
fake

## CONTEMPLATION

I wonder what cats think about
. . . They always look as though
they're planning
something

## HIGHER EDUCATION

Pain is very loyal
. . . Like the albatross
it stays tethered to us
even when we
let it
go . . . But

There is a moment
in all our lives when we
adjust our steps
to pace the
journey

. . . The game is partly twisted
by wisdom
. . . We get ahead
not by leaving people
but by getting closer
to them

. . . Time does not cure
loyalty
. . . It improves
it

# SOMEBODY I USED TO
# BE IN LOVE WITH

He's human again
. . . There's a bit of food
caught between his front teeth
and it has absolutely
no charm

There is no adventure
in listening to what he plans to do
with his life now
. . . His future without me
does not hold my
interest

What do you say to
somebody you used to
be in love
with?

He wants me to tell him one more time that
my Father would have loved him . . . He's lonesome
for the girl who could make him feel
that he could do
anything . . . Because

He's human again
. . . There's a burnt-orange color in his hair

A mixture of brown dye and
gray/compounded by the sun
It has absolutely
no charm . . . And

There is no blindness waiting
in the wine
anymore

## AN ARGUMENT FOR ABSOLUTION

He thinks his honesty
redeems him . . . He thinks
telling the truth
will change the
facts

He thinks confessing his crimes
and giving you their brutal details
will change everything
But
*Honesty has never*
*changed the*
*truth*

✦ ✦ ✦ ✦

# WHY WOMEN LIVE
# LONGER THAN MEN

"Don't fool yourself
about this," she said
"Men cook to eat" and
"Women always cook
for company"

Look at my Nana
. . . She didn't stop making gingerbread
after Pop was gone
. . . She always saved the end piece
and fed it to
the birds

. . . So I don't fool myself
about these things anymore
. . . I know there's a reason why
women live longer
than men

❁ ❁ ❁ ❁

# PRAYING FOR HUNGER

The younger men are coming up for your promises, Mary
Young men with no moods/no guilt/no gold in their
    teeth
They are so beautiful you cannot tell
them apart

They have no old music pressed into their eyes
they will give you white dresses and stars
you can stretch your mouth over them
in one bite

Pray for hunger, Mary
this is food/this is what grows
You can weep this pleasure in
there is birth on your instrument
hold him where he is held
You will feel no love for him
except this
yielding

These boys cannot be your heroes, Mary
Their love is too red and
they have no needles in their eyes

Pray for a mistake, Mary
go falling and
go fast

✿ ✿ ✿ ✿

---

# THE DISTANCE BETWEEN
# TWO PEOPLE

He lives across the street
And I measure off the block
at both ends
so that the whole neighborhood
can be our home
. . . He in one room
Me in another

*The distance between*
*any two people*
*is only the length*
*of their*
*arms*

## THE LIE THAT CAME TRUE

I said, "I'll miss you"
but, I didn't
then

How could I understand change
when my socks were always in the same drawer?
how could I know how to want you back
when you'd always been with me?

"I'll miss you," I said
. . . *it was a lie*
*that came*
*true*

# INTENTION

A promise is
just a
wish

A way to dream
out loud

Language is
only
intention

## HORSE SENSE

Everything has to do
with food of one kind
or another

# BACK TO THE BELLY

Ah Captain, take me on your travels
I am so tired of the wounded
so full of the land

I want to be a sailor
I cannot hold on to the shoreman
I am moored by their weeping
white is missing from everything

Ah Captain, let me be your second girl
I could ride your wild part/I can make up for hurting
    you last year
I could be your seawhore/I will let you be my wetboy
I will teach you to beg again
I will be your bible/Captain please/take me across the
    line
You can be a skinkiller
Give me your hardness and I will return your
childhood with fevers

Take me where I cannot leave you
we can untie the thick, brown knot and
unfold the dead end

You can give me everything I ever wanted in this one
    move
I can be your hand
I can be that part that moves you up and down

We can go back to the belly
I will bear you joy
I will birth you, Captain
I will let you come and
I will let you
go

# RESTRICTIONS

He thinks 'being strong'
is holding back
and hiding our feelings
when 'being strong' has always been
letting go and allowing our feelings
to be
felt

Internal bleeding is
always more
dangerous
. . . *Even joy becomes a burden*
*when you can't*
*laugh*

# OPENINGS

I fell towards his chest like something dropped
I had stones in my heart
my loneliness broke into little motors
and I sank back opening
opening

His mouth is an ocean/this Wednesday boy
He opens and opens/He comes around me in long/wet/
    warm/round waves
spreading me under him like an iron/flat/hot/soft
He eats my heart out
And I lay in his noise burning
joyfully to death

I can hear foghorns moaning
ships float unchained
heavy against heavy

I will never miss this man
and I will never forget
him

# THE HIGH HOLIDAYS

It's only when we're in love
or when we're little
that Christmas really comes true
. . . In between
it can break our hearts
with
expectation

## A CALL FROM HOME

I heard that song today
and I thought
of you

## FAMILY RESEMBLANCE

I've loved you deeper than anyone
I've ever loved in my life
I loved you like my Mother
loved him . . . It shouldn't surprise me
that I'm losing you so long
and so hard

I remember as a kid
My Mother left the porchlight on
all night
. . . I wish I would have kissed her
more often in the
morning

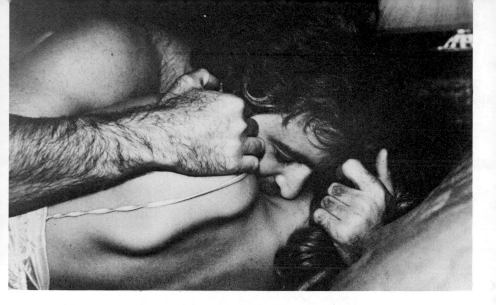

✺ ✺ ✺ ✺

## THE PLACE WHERE
## BABIES COME FROM

There is a place
Lower than birth
Below the seed
. . . It is where children
give birth to parents
. . . where the human is too true
to be good

It's the place
where babies come from

# THE FEAR OF *NOT* BEING SCARED

There is a great fear
that plagues only romantics
and children . . .
It is that they might
be alright
alone

## A MATTER OF FACT

It's amazing how many people
will care about you
if only you would care
about them . . . And

It's even more remarkable
how many people
will care about you
anyway

✹ ✹ ✹ ✹

# PRIVATE PRACTICES

We may all
get there . . . we may even
arrive at the
same time . . . But
we all
come
alone

✱ ✱ ✱ ✱

# THE LAST LAUGH

There are some people
who would rather be right
than happy
as though making a point
was more fun than
having a good
time

These are the people
who will risk their lives
to get the last laugh
even though it isn't
funny

# ABSURDITY

There are no illegitimate babies

❀ ❀ ❀ ❀

# ONE OF THE THINGS
# THAT HASN'T CHANGED

The best part of riding on a 'Merry-Go-Round'
Is waving to somebody who isn't
    riding on a
        'Merry-Go-Round'

# MAN AND HIS WEAPON

For centuries
man has been asking for peace
and *preparing* for war
. . . Man against men/military twins
Siblings of the same
author

Life has always been an *arms* race
Men in competition with man
obsessed with being *bigger*
and *better.* . . . Man and his weapon
Seed against seed/raging against
a final similarity

Men against *man*/A nuclear duet
Mirror against mirror/solitary twins
Guiding their muscles into
the same soil

War is just another kind
of jealousy

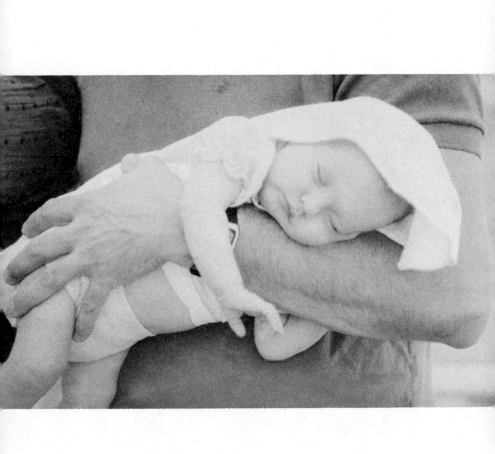

# MONTHLY PAYMENTS

Every month
I feel the soil turn within my belly
. . . My womb
that old veteran
faithfully cleans the earth
and waits

It has been a long time
since my body has celebrated around
the seed . . . I long to be more
intimate with nature . . . and
my breasts (those pink tables)
their craft is left for
pleasure . . .

Every month
the tissue forms around a prayer
and when it isn't answered
it turns to blood . . . and

Every time that happens
I hear a small requiem
in the southern part
of my belly

＊ ＊ ＊ ＊

# 5 AM IN SAUSALITO

It's 5 am in Sausalito
I am all dressed up beneath the northern sky
I came here in a rented car
I parked it right in front of Patterson's bar
where you used to kiss me
right in front of
everybody

Two Septembers back
I drove my own car a thousand miles
to this harbor
I brought you from the city across the Golden Gate
There was a blaze of salmon light
across the ceiling of the sky . . . Do you
remember the song that was
playing?

I love you much more this morning
than I ever did that afternoon
(even though you held hands with another girl
the night before my birthday)
So

I came back to Sausalito before the sun came up
I didn't want anybody to be here when I gave you back
I came here in a rented car but
I wore my Laura Ashley dress
just in case

# FLIGHT #5 TO JFK

Here I am again
strapped to my seat
like a child
my food served to me
in high
chairs . . .

I trust strangers more in the air
The gentleman beside me becomes a lifetime friend
in an hour . . . only to be lost again
in baggage claim

An airplane is just a small neighborhood
where women
take care of us like women
used to

I look out the window like a kid again
safely within another Mother
Travel has all the mysteries
of birth

Up here where no one lives
There is a lot of
living

✿ ✿ ✿ ✿

## OLD PHOTOGRAPHS

How often
do you think of all those people
who you were never
going to
forget?

# REQUIEM FOR A HEAVYWEIGHT

My friend Jack
went to Heaven this morning
Wally called and told me
that he left the house
around nine o'clock
. . . He should be there
by now

We knew he was leaving
Lately when he took our hand
he squeezed
a little harder
than he used
to

We were all in on it
Each of us had an awkward moment
when we laughed too loud
or tried too hard
He knew why we called more often
He knew why we stayed
a little longer
than we used
to

My friend Jack
Left a big hole in the world today
All three networks used the past tense

as they pointed out his triple crown
and poured him into
history . . . But

We knew he was getting ready
We were all in on it

## MAC

Mac is asleep now
growing wings
in her room

All fifteen years of her
are ready to come
true

All of her faces return to me
I remember especially
how she waited for me
behind that fence at the
nursery school
and how she ran to meet me at the gate
with her arms begging
"Hold me, Mama!"

It has been such a long time
since I have squeezed her in against my heart
. . . It will be longer still
until I can
again

Mac is growing wings tonight
I can see them coming
They will be larger than mine
They will lift her out ahead
of me

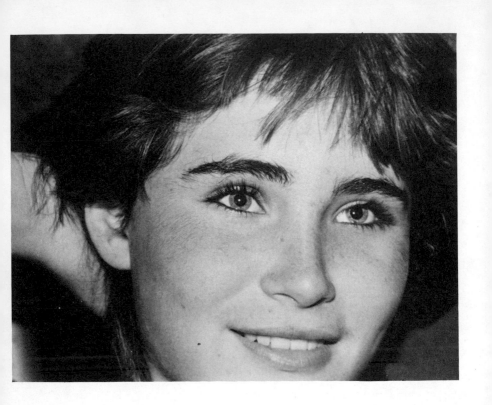

It is hard for me to imagine how far she will go
or how soon/It is something she is dreaming
now . . . So
I pulled up the quilt around her tonight
and I kissed her right where
she used to smile so much . . . on the voice that must
deny me
. . . I closed the light around us
It is time for us to be
foreigners

Mac is leaving me
It is that twist in nature that my own Mother
warned me about
. . . The next time I see her
she will be my
sister

. . . I can hardly wait
to be your friend
It has been so hard
to be your
keeper

Wherever you are when you read this page
wherever you're going from here
I want you to know that I'm still here
in the body where you
came from

I'm a woman, Mac
I carried the seeds like you do now
. . . I know how important it is for you
to come back to me before
you leave again a second and
final time

It's my turn to stay behind the fence

✸ ✸ ✸ ✸

## SILLY WILLY & CAITLIN P.

I feel closer to people
when they're silly
. . . I guess that's when I am reminded most
of what I liked about them
in the first place

# ❋ ❋ ❋ ❋

## KING OF THE 88s

When I first met Alexis
his hands looked just like everybody else's
I had yet to experience him
at a piano

It wasn't until tonight
in a concert hall
that his music was to separate him
from anyone else in
my memory

I never dreamed that one pair of hands
could touch so many people
at once

I always knew that Alexis was charming
His beauty became visible to me in simple conversation
I had already included him among my treasures
I knew he was a generous man
But I hadn't imagined the gift
that trembled from him
tonight

It isn't often that a performer
exchanges blood with an
audience

And I wanted Alexis to know he surprised me
so genuinely that I was left ashamed
that I did not know it
all along

I am resolved to imagine again
I hadn't expected to be so perfectly amazed
. . . I am only sorry that
I didn't dream it
first

## SOMETHING I OFTEN FORGET DURING THE DAY

The stars don't come out at night
. . . They have always been there

## LAND LOVER

Don't worry
. . . I'll find
you

There is an eastern lighthouse
in me
and

. . . Like any sailor
you'll have to reach the shore now and then
before you can safely
love the
sea

# THE THIEF WHO
# COULDN'T GET AWAY

I knew a man
who didn't come to see his children for years
. . . How inept a thief he was
to rob from himself like that
. . . Ironically
his punishment for this
was that the children loved him
anyway . . . And
it broke his heart

❀ ❀ ❀ ❀

## MIXED BLESSINGS

I don't give up on people
. . . Something in me
always hangs
on

Belief is a funny thing
. . . It lets people leave
But it doesn't let
them
go

✸ ✸ ✸ ✸

# NOISE

Give me your noise/he said
C'mon let me have it
I will kill you for it if you like
and I can pay you too

Give it over throw it up
squeeze it out—scratch it open
let it come
Go on it's just noise

One scream and it empties out
it's just red air/bad money and white lies
I don't want to ruin you
I just want your noise
I will kill you for it if you insist
but I can pay you too

❁ ❁ ❁ ❁

# THAT ONE MAN

There is always that one man
who you can't avoid
that one face that becomes the only
representative of
Heaven

Every woman who has ever been a girl
can tell you what I
mean

Salvation is something that we have to create
before we discover
God . . . And

There is always that one man
who will make your talent useless
That one hunger whose mouth cannot
be healed

You cannot be cured of music
after you've been on your
knees

Every woman who has ever been a girl
can tell you what I
mean

There are men so beautiful
that we have to love them
twice

# ALL THE WORDS
# I'VE EVER WRITTEN DOWN

Language is just a lot of hands
This is the wonder of words and their embarrassment
I have written whole books
*of not knowing*

I do not know what moves us
I cannot hold it still
I have blisters from trying to stay the same
What loves you is not the body
This is how we learn eternity
Time does not wear out

Nobody can steal Christmas
This is what Dickens tried to tell us
We cannot stop what is true

Everything I've ever written down is about this

✿ ✿ ✿ ✿

# INVENTORY

There are people who give
and there are people who receive
This is a partnership

You can turn a wall into a window
you can tear apart your clock
this is all I know about fools and kings
there are people who call
and there are people who will answer back
We are one of them

This can tear apart our clocks
this can turn our walls into windows
this is why we say 'always'

There are people who will not let you down
they show up exactly where you can see them
as distance is measured/you are
half

There are humans turned angels by your asking
This is what we can learn about fools and kings
There are people who will answer back
We are one of them